Contents

Some words are shown in bold, **like this**. You can find out what they mean by looking in the glossary.

Meet the spiders

Spiders are not **insects**.

Spiders are **arachnids**. They have eight legs and two main body parts. Most spiders have eight eyes. They do not have wings or **antennae**.

Autumn   Winter   Spring

LIFE CYCLE OF A...

Spider

Revised and Updated

Ron Fridell
and
Patricia Walsh

www.heinemannlibrary.co.uk
Visit our website to find out more information about Heinemann Library books.

To order:
☎ Phone +44 (0) 1865 888066
🖷 Fax +44 (0) 1865 314091
🖥 Visit www.heinemannlibrary.co.uk

Heinemann Library is an imprint of Capstone Global Library Limited, a company incorporated in England and Wales having its registered office at 7 Pilgrim Street, London, EC4V 6LB - Registered company number: 6695582

"Heinemann" is a registered trademark of Pearson Education Limited, under licence to Capstone Global Library Limited

Text © Capstone Global Library Limited 1998, 2009
Second edition first published in hardback and paperback in 2009
The moral rights of the proprietor have been asserted.

Edited by Adrian Vigliano, Harriet Milles, and Diyan Leake
Designed by Kimberly R. Miracle and Tony Miracle
Original illustrations ©Capstone Global Library Limited 1998, 2009
Illustrated by David Westerfield
Picture research by Tracy Cummins and Heather Mauldin
Originated by Chroma Graphics (Overseas) Pte. Ltd.
Printed in China by South China Printing Company Ltd.

ISBN 978 0431 99956 2 (hardback)
13 12 11 10 09
10 9 8 7 6 5 4 3 2 1

ISBN 978 0431 99974 6 (paperback)
13 12 11 10 09
10 9 8 7 6 5 4 3 2 1

British Library Cataloguing in Publication Data
Fridell, Ron.
  Life cycle of a spider. -- 2nd ed.
  1. Spiders--Life cycles--Juvenile literature.
  I. Title II. Spider III. Walsh, Patricia, 1951-
  595.4'4'156-dc22
A full catalogue record for this book is available from the British Library.

Acknowledgements
We would like to thank the following for permission to reproduce photographs: age fotostock p. **24** (©Larry F. Jernigan); Alamy pp. **20** (©Lawrence Stepanowicz), **25** (©Peter Arnold, Inc./Byron Jorjorian); Corbis pp. **6** (©Papilio/Steve Austin), **13** (©Ecoscene/Julie Meench), **15**, **29 top left** (©David Roseburg), **16** (©Papilio/Dennis Johnson), **18** (©Layne Kennedy), **19** (©Papilio/Jamie Harron); Getty Images p. **5** (©Jerry Driendl); ©Dwight Kuhn pp. **10**, **11**, **12**, **28 top right**, **28 bottom**; Photolibrary p. **23** (©Dinodia Dinodia); Photo Researchers Inc. pp. **17**, **29 top right** (©Millard H. Sharpe); Photoshot pp. **14** (©Bruce Coleman/Bob Grossington), **27** (©Jane Burton); Shutterstock pp. **4** (©Peter Gudella), **7**, **29 bottom** (©Norbert Rehm), **8**, **9**, **21**, **28 top left** (©Cathy Keifer), **22** (©John Lumb); troyb.com p. **26** (©Troy Bartlett).

Cover photograph of a garden spider reproduced with permission of Shutterstock (©Darrell Blake Courtney).

We would like to thank Michael Bright for his invaluable help in the preparation of this book.

Every effort has been made to contact copyright holders of material reproduced in this book. Any omissions will be rectified in subsequent printings if notice is given to the publisher.

Some spiders have a poisonous bite.

There are many kinds of spiders. They can live on high mountains or in deep caves. Some live in wet swamps and some in dry deserts.

Early summer

Late summer

Most homes have a few spiders living in them.

Spiders also live in houses and gardens. They live wherever there are **insects** for them to catch and eat.

Autumn

Winter

Spring

All spiders make **silk**. Some kinds of spiders use their silk to spin webs in the shape of a wheel. The spider in this book is a female garden spider.

Spiders make silk with special parts of their bodies, called **spinnerets**.

Early summer

Late summer

Egg sac

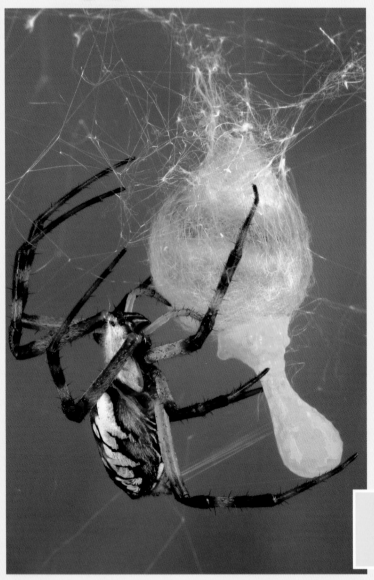

A spider begins its life as a tiny egg. A female spider lays hundreds of eggs.

The spider lays her eggs in the autumn.

Autumn

Winter

Spring

The female spider wraps the eggs in threads of **silk** to make a round, papery **egg sac**.

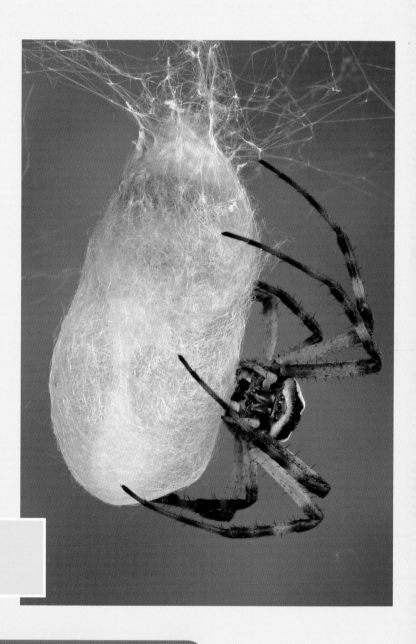

The spider hangs the egg sac in her web.

Hatching

This **egg sac** is full of tiny, baby spiders called spiderlings.

The eggs **hatch**. The **spiderling** is one of many baby spiders inside the egg sac. She stays inside with the others until the weather is warm.

Autumn

Winter

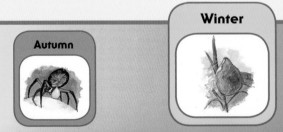

Spring

Most of the spiderlings escape from the egg sac at the same time.

Inside the egg sac, the spiderling grows. When she is ready to come out, she bites a tiny hole in the egg sac and escapes.

Spiderling

The **spiderlings** stay close together.

The new spiderling is tiny and white.
She stays with the other spiderlings in a
wiggling **cluster**.

Autumn

Winter

Spring

Only the strongest spiderlings will survive.

She will survive, but many spiderlings will not. They will be eaten by other hungry spiderlings.

Ballooning

The **spiderlings** must find new homes.

In a few days, the spiderling leaves the others. She climbs to the top of a grass stem or fence post to catch a **breeze**.

Autumn

Winter

Spring

The spiderling will make her new home wherever she lands.

The spiderling lets out **silk** from her **spinnerets**. The breeze tugs at the silk. The spiderling lifts off and flies on the wind. This is called **ballooning**.

Early summer

Late summer

15

Moulting

This young spider is growing bigger all the time.

The young spider hangs upside down from a **silk** thread. As she grows, her skin gets tight. She must get rid of her old skin. This is called **moulting**.

Autumn   Winter   Spring

Here you can see an old skin that a spider has just moulted.

The young spider's old skin splits along the sides of her body. Then she pulls her legs out of the skin.

New skin

The spider stretches and bends her legs to dry her new skin.

The spider's new skin is wrinkled and wet. When the new skin dries, it will be hard and will not stretch.

Autumn

Winter

Spring

The spider's new skin has dried and turned hard.

The young spider will grow and **moult** again. She will get a new skin five to nine times before she is an adult.

Early summer

Late summer

Spider

The **spiderling** is now a fully grown spider.

The spider spins her web in tall grass or in bushes. Each morning, she repairs any holes in the web. Then she sits in the middle of her web or hides nearby.

Autumn

Winter

Spring

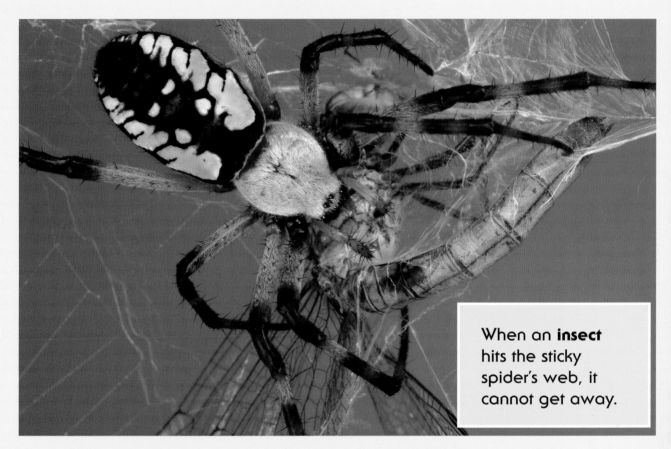

When an **insect** hits the sticky spider's web, it cannot get away.

The spider waits for an insect to get caught in the sticky web. When an insect is caught, the spider quickly wraps it in **silk** threads. She will eat the insect later.

Early summer

Late summer

Danger for spiders

The spider has to work hard every day to mend her web.

The spider's life is a hard one. Wind can rip her web. People spray **insecticides** that can kill the spider and the **insects** she eats.

Autumn

Winter

Spring

There is also danger from **predators**. Birds, wasps, frogs, lizards, and scorpions like to eat spiders.

A garden spider is a tasty treat for this bird.

Spider tricks

The spider does not get caught in her own web. A special claw on each foot helps her walk across her web without getting stuck.

The spider can move fast across her web.

Autumn

Winter

Spring

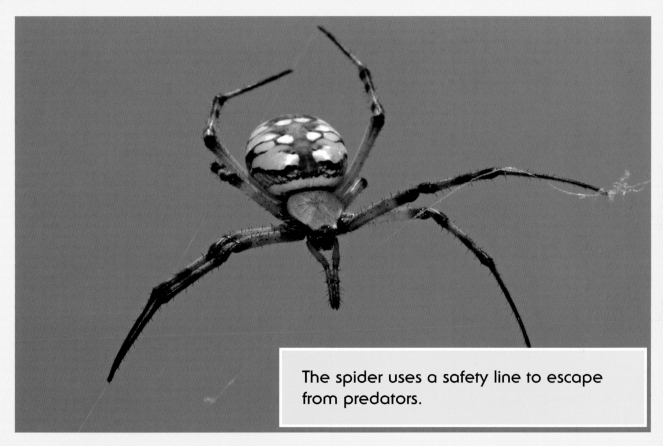

The spider uses a safety line to escape from predators.

When a **predator** comes near, the spider quickly spins a thread of **silk**. Then she drops off her web to escape.

Early summer

Late summer

Mating

Most male spiders are much smaller than the females.

The spider **mates** in early autumn. A male spider taps on the strings of the female's web to tell her he is near.

Autumn

Winter

Spring

The spiders have mated. Now the female is ready to lay her eggs.

After mating, the male spider's job is done, and he will die. The female spider will lay hundreds of eggs and make her **egg sacs**. Then she will die, too.

Early summer

Late summer

Life cycle

Egg sac

Hatching

Spiderling

Ballooning

Moulting

Adult spider

Fact file

- There are at least 38,000 different kinds of spiders. Scientists think there are many more to be discovered.

- Most spiders live from six months to two years. Big spiders, such as the tarantula, can live as long as twenty years.

- A tiny cave spider will lay only one egg, but some web-spinners will lay as many as 3,000 eggs.

- A female wolf spider carries her **egg sac** with her. A female burrowing spider hides her egg sac in a hole in the ground.

Glossary

antenna (More than one are called antennae.) long, thin feeler on an insect's head

arachnid animal with eight legs and two body parts (You say ah-RACK-nid.)

ballooning flying on a silk thread that is being blown by the wind

breeze light wind

cluster group

egg sac bag made by the female spider to hold her eggs

hatch break out of an egg

insect small animal that has six legs, a body with three main parts, and wings

insecticide poison that kills insects

mate when a male and female come together to make babies

moult shed the outer skin to allow the spider to grow

predator animal that eats other animals

repair fix something

silk thin, strong, and soft thread made by spiders

spiderling baby spider

spinneret finger-like part on the end of a spider's body that spins the silk threads

More books to read

Bug Books: Spider, Karen Hartley, Chris Macro, Philip Taylor (Heinemann Library, 2008)

Investigate: Life Cycles, Charlotte Guillain and Sue Barraclough (Heinemann Library, 2008)

How Living Things Grow: From Egg to Spider, Anita Ganeri (Heinemann Library, 2006)

Index